SIMPLE SCARVES
Made with the Knook™

Knooking is the new knitting!

The Knook is a specialized crochet hook that creates true knitted fabric, while the attached cord completely prevents dropped stitches! Use the Knook to make these 9 ribbed scarves quickly and easily. Clear instructions on the basic technique start on page 21, and are included for both right-hand & left-hand stitching, while photos illustrate each step. You'll also find excellent videos at LeisureArts.com that show every stitch step-by-step. Great for beginners or anyone who would like to learn to knit the easy way—the Knook makes knitting fun!

Get more! Visit LeisureArts.com for additional Knook pattern books, easy instructions, and our clear how-to videos! Look for the Knook at your local retailer or LeisureArts.com!

TABLE OF CONTENTS

LEISURE ARTS, INC.
Little Rock, Arkansas

2X2 RIB SCARF

◖◻◻◻ **BEGINNER**

Finished Size: Approximately 5" wide x 56" long (12.5 cm x 142 cm)

MATERIALS

Medium Weight Yarn **MEDIUM 4**
[3 ounces, 185 yards
(85 grams, 170 meters) per skein]:
  2 skeins
Knook, size H (5 mm)

SCARF

Ch 46.

Foundation Row: Pick up 45 sts on foundation ch: 46 sts.

Row 1 (Right side)**:** K2, (P2, K2) across.

Row 2: P2, (K2, P2) across.

Repeat Rows 1 and 2 for pattern until Scarf measures approximately 56" (142 cm) from foundation ch edge, ending by working Row 2.

Bind off all sts in pattern.

BEADED RIB SCARF

Finished Size: Approximately 5½" wide x 58" long (14 cm x 147.5 cm)

MATERIALS

Medium Weight Yarn **4**
[3 ounces, 185 yards
(85 grams, 170 meters) per skein]:
2 skeins
Knook, size H (5 mm)

SCARF

Ch 43.

Foundation Row: Pick up 42 sts on foundation ch: 43 sts.

Row 1 (Right side)**:** K1, P1, K1, (P2, K1, P1, K1) across.

Row 2: P3, (K2, P3) across.

Repeat Rows 1 and 2 for pattern until Scarf measures approximately 58" (147.5 cm) from foundation ch edge, ending by working Row 2.

Bind off all sts in pattern.

CARTRIDGE RIB SCARF

■□□□ **BEGINNER**

Finished Size: Approximately 5½" wide x 54" long (14 cm x 137 cm)

MATERIALS
Medium Weight Yarn 🧶 **4**
[3 ounces, 185 yards
(85 grams, 170 meters) per skein]:
   2 skeins
Knook, size H (5 mm)

SCARF
Ch 42.

Foundation Row: Pick up 41 sts on foundation ch: 42 sts.

Row 1: K3, P1, (K4, P1) across to last 3 sts, K3.

Row 2 (Right side)**:** P2, (K3, P2) across.

Repeat Rows 1 and 2 for pattern until Scarf measures approximately 54" (137 cm) from foundation ch edge, ending by working Row 1.

Bind off all sts in pattern.

MISTAKE RIB SCARF

Finished Size: Approximately 5½" wide x 51" long
(14 cm x 129.5 cm)

MATERIALS
Medium Weight Yarn **MEDIUM 4**
[3 ounces, 185 yards
85 grams 170 meters per skein]:
  2 skeins
Knook, size H (5 mm)

SCARF
Ch 43.

Foundation Row: Pick up 42 sts on foundation ch:
43 sts.

Row 1: K2, (P2, K2) across to last st, P1.

Repeat Row 1 for pattern until Scarf measures
approximately 51" (129.5 cm) from foundation ch
edge.

Bind off all sts in pattern.

TEXTURED RIB SCARF

Finished Size: Approximately 5" wide x 62" long
(12.5 cm x 157.5 cm)

MATERIALS
Medium Weight Yarn ⓜ④
[3 ounces, 185 yards
(85 grams, 170 meters) per skein]:
   2 skeins
Knook, size H (5 mm)

SCARF
Ch 41.

Foundation Row: Pick up 40 sts on foundation ch: 41 sts.

Row 1 (Right side)**:** K2, P2, K1, P2, (K3, P2, K1, P2) across to last 2 sts, K2.

Row 2: P2, K2, P1, K2, (P3, K2, P1, K2) across to last 2 sts, P2.

Rows 3 and 4: Repeat Rows 1 and 2.

Row 5: K1, (P2, K3, P2, K1) across.

Row 6: P1, (K2, P3, K2, P1) across.

Rows 7 and 8: Repeat Rows 5 and 6.

Repeat Rows 1-8 for pattern until Scarf measures approximately 62" (157.5 cm) from foundation ch edge, ending by working Row 8.

Bind off all sts in pattern.

TWIN RIB SCARF

Finished Size: Approximately 6" wide x 54½" long (15 cm x 138.5 cm)

MATERIALS

Medium Weight Yarn **(4)**
[3 ounces, 185 yards
(85 grams, 170 meters) per skein]:
  2 skeins
Knook, size H (5 mm)

SCARF
Ch 42.

Foundation Row: Pick up 41 sts on foundation ch: 42 sts.

Row 1 (Right side)**:** (K3, P3) across.

Row 2: (K1, P1) across.

Repeat Rows 1 and 2 for pattern until Scarf measures approximately 54½" (138.5 cm) from foundation ch edge, ending by working Row 2.

Bind off all sts in pattern.

WAVY RIB SCARF

Finished Size: Approximately 6¼" wide x 59" long
(16 cm x 150 cm)

MATERIALS

Medium Weight Yarn **(4)** MEDIUM
[3 ounces, 185 yards
(85 grams, 170 meters) per skein]:
2 skeins
Knook, size H (5 mm)

SCARF

Ch 44.

Foundation Row: Pick up 43 sts on foundation ch: 44 sts.

Row 1 (Right side)**:** P2, (K4, P2) across.

Row 2: K2, (P4, K2) across.

Rows 3-6: Repeat Rows 1 and 2 twice.

Row 7: K3, P2, (K4, P2) across to last 3 sts, K3.

Row 8: P3, K2, (P4, K2) across to last 3 sts, P3.

Rows 9-12: Repeat Rows 7 and 8 twice.

Repeat Rows 1-12 for pattern until Scarf measures approximately 59" (150 cm) from foundation ch edge, ending by working Row 12.

Bind off all sts in pattern.

WAFFLE STITCH SCARF

○○○○ **BEGINNER**

Finished Size: Approximately 5" wide x 56" long
(12.5 cm x 142 cm)

MATERIALS
Medium Weight Yarn **(4)** MEDIUM
[3 ounces, 185 yards
(85 grams, 170 meters) per skein]:
    2 skeins
Knook, size H (5 mm)

SCARF
Ch 40.

Foundation Row: Pick up 39 sts on foundation ch: 40 sts.

Row 1 (Right side)**:** P1, (K2, P1) across.

Row 2: K1, (P2, K1) across.

Row 3: P1, (K2, P1) across.

Row 4: Knit across.

Repeat Rows 1-4 for pattern until Scarf measures approximately 56" (142 cm) from foundation ch edge, ending by working Row 3.

Bind off all sts in **knit**.

KNIT AND RIB SCARF

Finished Size: Approximately 5½" wide x 54" long (14 cm x 137 cm)

MATERIALS
Medium Weight Yarn 【4】
[3 ounces, 185 yards
(85 grams, 170 meters) per skein]:
  2 skeins
Knook, size H (5 mm)

SCARF
Ch 42.

Foundation Row: Pick up 41 sts on foundation ch: 42 sts.

Row 1 (Right side)**:** Purl across.

Row 2: (P3, K1, P1, K1) across.

Row 3: (P3, K3) across.

Rows 4-6: Repeat Rows 2 and 3 once, then repeat Row 2 once **more**.

Row 7: Purl across.

Row 8: (K1, P1, K1, P3) across.

Row 9: (K3, P3) across.

Rows 10-12: Repeat Rows 8 and 9 once, then repeat Row 8 once **more**.

Repeat Rows 1-12 for pattern until Scarf measures approximately 54" (137 cm) from foundation ch edge, ending by working Row 6 or Row 12.

Bind off all sts in **purl**.

GENERAL INSTRUCTIONS

ABBREVIATIONS

ch(s)	chain(s)
cm	centimeters
K	knit
mm	millimeters
P	purl
st(s)	stitch(es)

( ) or [ ] — work enclosed instructions as many times as specified by the number immediately following or work all enclosed instructions in the stitch or space indicated or contains explanatory remarks.

colon (:) — the number(s) given after a colon at the end of a row or round denote(s) the number of stitches you should have on that row or round.

front vs. **back** side — As you are working, the side facing you is the **front** of your work; the **back** is the side away from you.

right vs. **wrong** side — On the finished piece, the right side of your work is the side that the public will see.

KNOOK TERMINOLOGY	
UNITED STATES	**INTERNATIONAL**
gauge =	tension
bind off =	cast off
yarn over (YO) =	yarn forward (yfwd) **or** yarn around needle (yrn)

Yarn Weight Symbol & Names	SUPER FINE 1	FINE 2	LIGHT 3	MEDIUM 4	BULKY 5	SUPER BULKY 6
Type of Yarns in Category	Sock, Fingering Baby	Sport, Baby	DK, Light Worsted	Worsted, Afghan, Aran	Chunky, Craft, Rug	Bulky, Roving
Knook Gauge Ranges in Stockinette St to 4" (10 cm)	27-32 sts	23-26 sts	21-24 sts	16-20 sts	12-15 sts	6-11 sts
Advised Knook Size Range	B-1 to D-3	D-3 to F-5	F-5 to G-6	G-6 to I-9	I-9 to K-10½	M-13 and larger

■□□□ **BEGINNER**	Projects for first-time stitchers using basic knit and purl stitches. Minimal shaping.
■■□□ **EASY**	Projects using basic stitches, repetitive stitch patterns, simple color changes, knitting in the round techniques, and simple shaping and finishing.
■■■□ **INTERMEDIATE**	Projects with a variety of stitches, such as basic cables and lace, simple intarsia, and mid-level shaping and finishing.
■■■■ **EXPERIENCED**	Projects using advanced techniques and stitches, such as short rows, fair isle, more intricate intarsia, cables, lace patterns, and numerous color changes.

KNOOK BASICS

Using the Knook to create amazing knitted projects is fun and so easy! Let our step-by-step Basic Instructions show you how it's done. They're written and photographed for both left- and right-hand knooking. You'll get off to a fast start and be ready to create any of these beautiful scarves. Be sure to visit LeisureArts.com to see the video versions of these instructions—every stitch and technique in this book is there, plus a few more! You'll also find free patterns for more Knook designs!

KNOOK PREP
Thread the cord through the hole at the end of the Knook. Gently pull the cord so that one end is approximately 8" (20.5 cm) from the Knook *(Fig. A)*, leaving a long end.

Fig. A

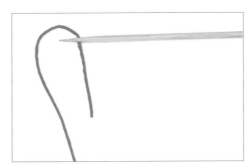

HOLDING THE KNOOK

There are two ways to hold the Knook. Hold the Knook as you would hold a pencil (*Fig. B*), or as you would grasp a table knife (*Fig. C*). Find the manner that is most comfortable for you.

Fig. B
Right-handed

Left-handed

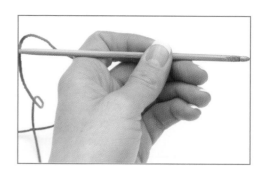

Fig. C
Right-handed

Left-handed

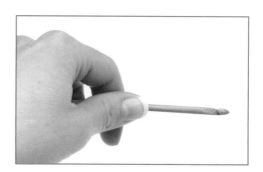

SLIP KNOT

The first step is to make a slip knot. Pull a length of yarn from the skein and make a circle approximately 8" (20.5 cm) from the end and place it on top of the yarn. The yarn on the skein-side of the circle is the working yarn, the opposite end is the yarn tail.

Slip the Knook under the yarn in the center of the circle *(Fig. D)*, then pull on both ends to tighten *(Fig. E)*.

Fig. D
Right-handed

Left-handed

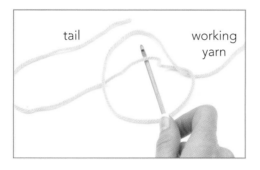

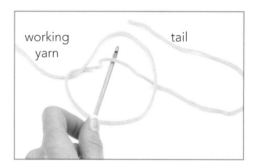

Fig. E
Right-handed

Left-handed

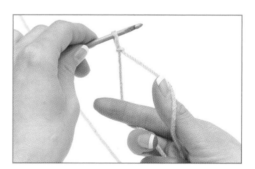

FOUNDATION CHAIN

Once the slip knot is on the Knook, the next step is to chain the required number of stitches, which is called the foundation chain.

With the Knook in your preferred hand, hold the slip knot with your thumb and middle finger of your other hand. Loop the working yarn over your index finger, grasping it in your palm to help control the tension of your yarn as you work the stitches *(Fig. F)*.

Fig. F
Right-handed

Left-handed

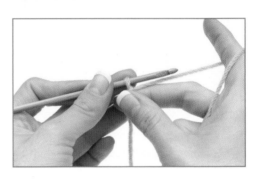

Wrap the yarn around the Knook from **back** to **front** *(Fig. G)*.

Fig. G
Right-handed

Left-handed

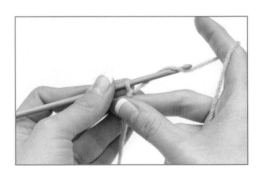

Turn the Knook to catch the yarn and draw the yarn through the slip knot *(Fig. H)*. Each time you wrap the yarn and draw the yarn through, you make one chain *(abbreviated ch)* of the foundation chain.

Fig. H
Right-handed

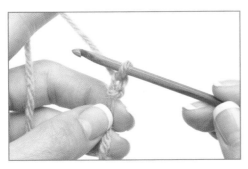

Left-handed

Repeat these steps to make the required number of chains.

If you already know how to crochet, please study the photos closely. From this point on, you will **NOT** be using the same yarn over typically used in crochet.

PICKING UP STITCHES

The loop on your Knook counts as the first stitch *(abbreviated st)*. To pick up the next stitch, insert the Knook from **front** to **back** into the second chain from the Knook *(Fig. I)*.

Fig. I
Right-handed

Left-handed

With the Knook facing down, catch the yarn *(Fig. J)* and pull the yarn through the chain *(Fig. K)*. Repeat until you have picked up a stitch in each chain across *(Fig. L)*.

Fig. J
Right-handed

Left-handed

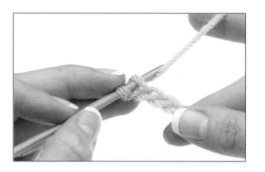

Fig. K
Right-handed

Left-handed

Fig. L
Right-handed

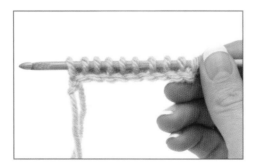

Left-handed

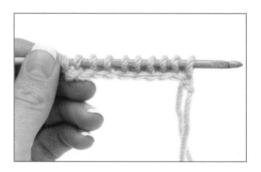

Slide the stitches off the Knook onto the cord *(Fig. M)*, allowing the short end to hang freely *(Fig. N)*.

Fig. M
Right-handed

Left-handed

Fig. N
Right-handed

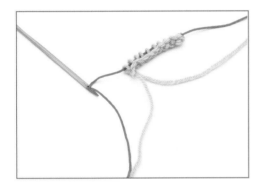

Left-handed

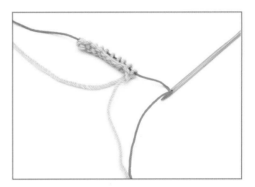

Turn your work around so that the working yarn and the yarn tail are closest to the Knook (*Fig. O*).

Fig. O
Right-handed

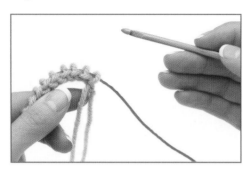

Left-handed

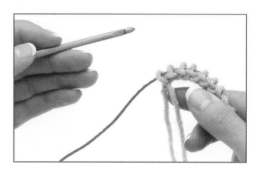

With the Knook in your preferred hand, hold your work with your other hand. Loop the working yarn over your index finger (*Fig. P*).

Fig. P
Right-handed

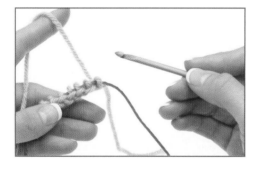

Left-handed

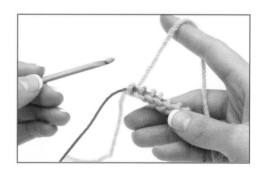

KNIT STITCH
Hold the work with the yarn to the **back**.

For right-handers, insert the Knook from **left** to **right** into the first stitch *(Fig. Q)*.

Fig. Q
Right-handed

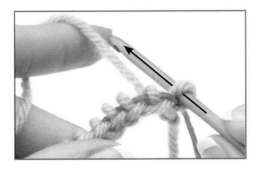

For left-handers, insert the Knook from **right** to **left** into the first stitch *(Fig. Q)*.

Fig. Q
Left-handed

With the Knook facing down, catch the yarn *(Fig. R)* and pull it through the stitch, forming a knit stitch on the Knook *(Fig. S)*.

Fig. R
Right-handed

Left-handed

Fig. S
Right-handed

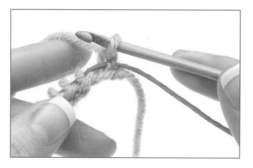

Left-handed

Keeping the yarn to the **back** of your work, repeat this process for each stitch across. Count the stitches to make sure you have the same number of stitches *(Fig. T)*.

Fig. T
Right-handed

Left-handed

If you do not have the required number of stitches, it is very easy to fix it at this point. Simply pull the Knook back out in the opposite direction you were working until you get to the mistake, and pull the yarn to undo the stitches.

Once each stitch has been worked, gently pull the long end of the cord out of the work, leaving the new stitches on the Knook *(Fig. U)*.

Fig. U
Right-handed

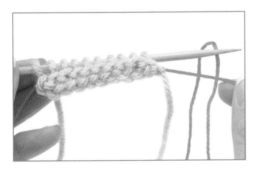

Left-handed

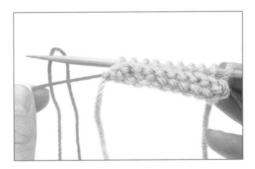

Slide the stitches off the Knook onto the long end of the cord, then turn the work.

PURL STITCH
Hold the work with the yarn to the **front**.

For right-handers, insert the Knook into the stitch from **right** to **left** *(Fig. V)*.

Fig. V
Right-handed

For left-handers, insert the Knook into the stitch from **left** to **right** *(Fig. V)*.

Fig. V
Left-handed

With the Knook facing away from you, wrap the yarn from **front** to **back** (*Fig. W*).

Fig. W
Right-handed

Left-handed

Catch the yarn with the Knook and pull the yarn through the stitch forming a purl stitch on the Knook (*Fig. X*). Keeping the yarn to the **front** of your work, repeat this process for each stitch across.

Once each stitch has been worked, gently pull the long end of the cord out of the work, leaving the new stitches on the Knook.

Fig. X
Right-handed

Left-handed

Slide the stitches off the Knook onto the long end of the cord, then turn the work.

Working the knit stitch on every row creates a fabric called Garter Stitch. You will also create Garter Stitch if you purl every row.

Garter Stitch

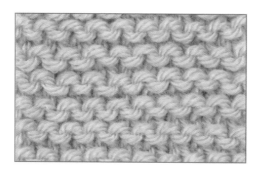

If you alternate knitting one row, then purling one row, the resulting knitted fabric is called Stockinette Stitch.

Stockinette Stitch
(right side)

Stockinette Stitch
(wrong side)

BIND OFF
Binding off is the method used to remove and secure your stitches from the Knook cord so that they won't unravel.

To bind off all the stitches in knit, knit the first two stitches *(Fig. Y)*. Pull the second stitch through the first stitch.

Fig. Y
Right-handed

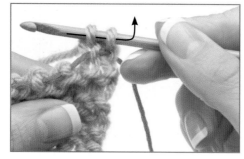

Left-handed

One stitch should remain on the Knook (*Fig. Z*). Knit the next stitch and pull it through the stitch on the Knook.

Fig. Z
Right-handed

Left-handed

Repeat this process until there are no stitches on the cord and only one stitch remains on the Knook (*Fig. AA*).

Fig. AA
Right-handed

Left-handed

Pull the cord out of the work. Cut the yarn, leaving a long end to weave in later. Slip the remaining stitch off the Knook, pull the end through the stitch, and tighten the stitch.

To bind off in pattern, knit or purl the first two stitches as indicated for the pattern, pulling the second stitch through the first stitch as illustrated above and continuing across until all stitches are bound off.

YARN INFORMATION

The Scarves in this leaflet were made using NaturallyCaron.com Country. Any brand of Medium Weight yarn may be used. It is best to refer to the yardage/meters when determining how many balls or skeins to purchase. Remember, to achieve the same look, it is the weight of yarn that is important, not the brand of yarn.

For your convenience, listed below are the specific colors used to create our photography models.

2 X 2 RIB SCARF
#0007 Naturally

TWIN RIB SCARF
#0008 Silver Service

BEADED RIB SCARF
#0011 Gilded Age

WAVY RIB SCARF
#0005 Ocean Spray

CARTRIDGE RIB SCARF
#0006 Berry Frappe

WAFFLE STITCH SCARF
#0021 Peacock

MISTAKE RIB SCARF
#0015 Deep Taupe

KNIT AND RIB SCARF
#0018 Spice House

TEXTURED RIB SCARF
#0012 Foliage

We have made every effort to ensure that these instructions are accurate and complete. We cannot, however, be responsible for human error, typographical mistakes, or variations in individual work.

Production Team: Technical Writer/Editor - Sarah J. Green; Editorial Writer - Susan McManus Johnson; Senior Graphic Artist - Lora Puls; Graphic Artist - Becca Snider; Photo Stylists - Brooke Duszota and Sondra Daniel; and Photographers - Jason Masters and Ken West.